T0210123

REDISCOVERING UNCHANGING LOVE

MIHAI COCEA

WESTBOW
PRESS®
A DIVISION OF THOMAS NELSON
& ZONDERVAN

WestBow Press books may be ordered through booksellers or by contacting:

WestBow Press
A Division of Thomas Nelson & Zondervan
1663 Liberty Drive
Bloomington, IN 47403
www.westbowpress.com
1 (866) 928-1240

Scripture taken from the King James Version of the Bible.

ISBN: 978-1-9736-9205-8 (sc)
ISBN: 978-1-9736-9206-5 (e)

Library of Congress Control Number: 2020909416

Print information available on the last page.

WestBow Press rev. date: 06/04/2020

May your heart sing and your life explode with the joys of knowing the fullness of His unchanging love that lies potentially before you.

Contents

Introduction ix

The Cases of the Old Testament

The Case of Elijah and Elisha 1
The Case of Moses 6
Additions to Elisha's Case 12
The Case of Abraham 15
The Case of Job 18
The Case of Samuel 22
The Case of Uzzah 26
The Case of King Josiah 28
The Case of Ezekiel 30

The Cases of the New Testament

The Case of the New Church 35
The Case of Paul 39
The Case of the Eternal Fire 42

Paying Close Attention to the Words Is Crucial 45
Elijah the Legacy 48
Addendum 55

Introduction

When Adam and Eve chose to eat from the forbidden fruit, humankind began to fear God. He has always been misunderstood. Many verses from the Bible seem to contradict the ever-loving character of God, and most people consider His love a mystery that changed drastically from the Old Testament to the new. Apostle James declared in James 1:17 that with God there, "is no variableness, neither shadow of turning." He simply says that God does not change. Malachi writes the same thing in Malachi 3:6: "For I am the Lord, I change not." For this reason, I have decided to present and explain some of the misunderstandings and contradictions on which many have stumbled. And by God's grace, I will try to help fulfill in part Zacharia's prophecy concerning the work of Christ as declared in Luke 1:74: "that we being delivered out of the hand of our enemies might serve Him without fear."

THE CASES OF
THE OLD TESTAMENT

The Case of Elijah and Elisha

Elisha was Elijah's disciple and took his place after Elijah was taken to heaven. Everyone in Israel knew that Elisha was ordained by God to be a prophet in Elijah's place.

One day at the beginning of Elisha's career, he was on his way to Bethel when a group of little children met him and mocked him. It was obvious that the children were not educated in the ways of the Lord, and their mockery infuriated the prophet. "He turned back, and looked on them, and cursed them in the name of the Lord. And there came forth two she bears out of the wood, and tare forty and two children of them" (2 Kings 2:23–24).

To be able to understand what happened, imagine this account in the New Testament. Imagine yourself as a Christian sent by the Lord on a mission and being mocked for your religion by a group of children. Feeling offended by their mockery, you curse them in the name of Jesus and set two big dogs on them. Would that be approved in the eyes of the Lord? Would He say, "Well done, my faithful servant"? Obviously not. The character of the God who set the bears on those children does not match the character of Jesus. If we agree that Jesus is God (Titus 2:13), then we agree that Jesus was also the God of the Old Testament. Therefore, it is safe to say that Jesus is the God that could've set the bears on those children. But there's something in my heart that makes me think this is impossible. How could the same God that invited the children to come to Him (Matt.

19:14) do this? This is where we have to let the Bible explain this mystery. We have to let the Bible explain itself.

In the Bible we have a similar case that is part of the key to a sound interpretation of this story. Second Samuel 24:1 and 1 Chronicles 21:1 have different descriptions of King David's census. Let's look at 2 Samuel 24:1. It says, "And again the anger of the Lord was kindled against Israel, and he moved David against them to say, Go, number Israel and Judah." Now we will look at 1 Chronicles 21:1, which says, "And Satan stood up against Israel, and provoked David to number Israel." Everybody knows that it is a sin to number God's people (2 Sam. 24:10; 1 Chron. 21:6). If that is the case, then David is being tempted to commit a sin. We also know that the work of Satan is to tempt people to sin. But what about God? Does He tempt people to sin? Did He tempt David to number Israel? We have a verse that clears this confusion. That verse is James 1:13, which says, "Let no man say when he is tempted, I am tempted of God: for God cannot be tempted with evil, neither tempteth he any man." This verse is a law for God, and it states clearly that God does not tempt and that He has never tempted anybody. Therefore, we can safely conclude that 2 Samuel 24:1 must be wrong, not that there's a mistake in this verse, but that God allowed it to be written in such way so that it can be used as an important key to interpreting similar situations. So even though the verse says that it was God who tempted David to do the census, it was actually Satan acting as God. The person who wrote that verse thought that it was God. In the New Testament Paul says that "Satan himself is transformed into an angel of light" (2 Cor. 11:14). He can obviously make himself look like God too.

A similar case is when King Saul went to the witch of Endor (1 Sam. 28:3–20). He went to her so that through her he might be able to communicate with Samuel, who was dead. During that encounter, the witch, apparently, brings Samuel's spirit from the dead. The Bible says that the spirit that came was Samuel himself. It says in verse 15, "And Samuel said to Saul, Why hast thou disquieted me, to bring me up?" If we read the entire context, paying attention to the words of Samuel, we realize that the spirit is not Samuel. First of all, how can a witch dare to call on the spirit of God's prophet? Second, if this is truly the righteous Samuel, then why doesn't he rebuke Saul for going to a witch, contrary to God's commandment? This spirit mentions nothing about Saul's persecutions against David. Saul swore in the name of the Lord that he wouldn't kill David, and he trespassed it (1 Sam. 19:6). He also killed God's priests of Nob, along with the women and children in that city, and "Samuel" makes no mention of it. From this careful study, we can safely conclude that even though the Bible says that the spirit was Samuel, it actually wasn't Samuel. The same Bible says in Ecclesiastes 9:5, "the dead know not anything."

Going back to the case of Elisha, we can be sure that the God of Israel, namely Jesus, did not set the two bears to kill the forty-two children. It was the devil himself. He saw the opportunity, and he acted quickly to make Elisha boast in revenge of his hurt ego and also to inflict terror in the hearts of all those who heard or read of this awful event. Satan succeeded in giving God a bad name, thanks to the prophet Elisha. Jesus also taught us not to curse but to bless even our enemies, especially children. Elisha needs to learn this.

From whom did Elisha learn this? From his master, Elijah. And this we must prove.

Right before Elijah was taken to heaven, Elisha was with him on top of a hill. This account is found in 2 Kings chapter 1. Previously, the Lord had sent Elijah to rebuke King Ahaziah for inquiring the god of Ekron about his recovery. This was condemned by the law of Moses. Elijah sent a message through the King's messengers that because he neglected to ask the God of Israel, he will die—according to the angel of the Lord. King Ahaziah was offended by Elijah's message and sent fifty men with captains to get Elijah.

When the captain finds Elijah, he behaves very arrogantly with him and says, "Thou man of God, the king hath said, Come down" (2 Kings 1:9). Let us not forget that Elijah was considered a pagan to the idolaters. It's as if someone today said, "You son of the devil, follow me!" According to the following verses, it seems that Elijah was very offended by the two captains. He asks God indirectly to send fire upon both groups of soldiers, and the fire consumed them. He answered them kind of like this: "Don't you know who I am and what I'm capable of?" The third captain and his fifty soldiers find mercy from Elijah because the captain behaved humbly. In verse 15, the angel of the Lord tells Elijah to go down with him and not to be afraid of him.

We shouldn't forget that the Lord taught Elijah a lesson at Mount Horeb in 1 Kings 19:9–13. There the Lord passed by, and a great wind blew before the Lord: "but the Lord was not in the wind: and after the wind an earthquake; but the Lord was not in the earthquake: and after the earthquake a fire; but the Lord was not in the fire: and after the fire a still small voice."

So here we can agree that the Lord did not send the fire to consume those soldiers because He is not about fire; it's not in His character. Sure, He sent fire to consume the sacrifice that Solomon prepared for the inauguration of the temple, but that fire didn't hurt anyone (2 Chron. 7:1). Besides, there is another similar account in the New Testament, in Luke 9:51–56, where Jesus's disciples James and John saw that the Samaritans rejected Jesus when He was on His way to Jerusalem. Seeking revenge for the sake of Jesus, they asked Jesus if they should command fire to come down from heaven and consume them. Jesus rebuked them and said, "Ye know not what manner of spirit ye are of. For the Son of man is not come to destroy men's lives, but to save them." So if that is the case with the disciples, then what makes Elijah's case any different? This simply means and explains that if anybody is seeking revenge, he is seeking it without the Lord's approval. Therefore, it is not from God's spirit but from the spirit of the devil. It is safe to say that the devil killed those soldiers with fire at Elijah's request and also those forty-two children because of Elisha's curse. Also, both captains asked Elijah to come down with them. In Matthew 5:41, Jesus said that if anybody, "shall compel thee to go a mile, go with him twain." Elijah shouldn't have been afraid to go with them.

How can this be? How can the Lord allow the devil to give Him a bad name? Through these terrifying actions, the Lord allowed the devil to inflict terror in the hearts of billions of people who wanted to approach the name of God; because He said that He is "merciful and gracious, longsuffering and abundant in goodness and truth" (Ex. 34:6, 7). Let us not forget that Elijah was taken to heaven soon after that incident, and we also see him with Moses on the Mount of Transfiguration, talking with Jesus about, "his decease which he should accomplish at Jerusalem" (Luke 9:28–31). What this actually means is that salvation is by grace. Elijah did not deserve eternal life, yet he received it by the grace of God, whom he loved with his whole heart, even though he couldn't fully grasp God's love for humankind, especially sinners and His enemies.

Believe it or not, he actually learned this from Moses. In the next chapters we analyze what actually inspired Elijah, Elisha, and others to think that seeking revenge is justifiable in the eyes of God.

The Case of Moses

Through Moses, God set the foundation of the standard of morality. God gave us through Moses the Ten Commandments, or the moral law, and the ceremonial law or system that pertained to the temple service. The ceremonial system was made up of laws and ordinances that were symbols that spoke about important things or events to come. The sacrifices, the temple, the priesthood, the Levitical order, and the feasts were all prophetical symbols that were fulfilled in Christ. Through his writings, he taught the people how to have a relationship with God and with each other.

Even though Moses set the standard for morality and true worship, in Ezekiel 20:25 I found a statement that is very surprising. Referring to the time when God's people spent forty years in the wilderness, God tells Ezekiel, "Wherefore I gave them also statutes that were not good, and judgments whereby they should not live." What this verse is saying is that some bad teachings were slipped through on purpose and used as stumbling blocks or snares to trap the hypocrite. This we must demonstrate.

In Matthew 5:31 and 32, Jesus gave a part of His most famous sermon, the Sermon on the Mount, and this is what He said, "It has been said (through Moses), whosoever shall put away his wife, let him give her a writing of divorcement: But I say unto you (meaning that there needs to be a change), that whosoever shall put away his wife, saving for the cause of fornication, causeth her to commit adultery: and whosoever shall marry her that is divorced commiteth adultery."

In Matthew 19:3–9, Jesus is giving instructions on the same issue. The Pharisees asked Him, "Why did Moses then command to give a writing of divorcement, and to put her away?" Jesus answered them, "Moses because of the hardness of your hearts suffered you to put away your wives: but from the beginning it was not so." Many stumbled over this commandment. Even many good people had to be taught a lesson because they stumbled over this teaching, people like David and Solomon and many others who had many wives.

What is going on? If this is a bad commandment that obviously needs to be changed, how did it slip through? The key is because of the hardening of their hearts. For the forty years that they spent in the wilderness, the Hebrews have always complained and rebelled against Moses and God. They've always refused to listen and to believe, meaning that they've always rejected God. When you reject to do the will of God, your heart hardens. God doesn't force anyone to do His will. If they refused to listen to Him, then He let them listen to the one they love, the father of rebellion, Satan. This is why God allowed Satan to teach some things, "which were not good and judgments whereby they should not live." They asked for it, and now they can have it.

Did this make Moses a bad prophet? Absolutely not. God allowed it, and it is a snare only for the hypocrite. Moses had no idea what was going on.

Moses also said, "An eye for an eye, and a tooth for a tooth." And this is what Jesus said about it: "But I say unto you, That ye resist not evil: but whosoever shall smite thee on thy right cheek, turn to him the other also" (Matt. 5:38, 39). If Jesus taught the exact opposite, this means that He changed it. If He changed it, that means it wasn't good for humankind. This is what inspired Elijah and Elisha to seek vengeance in the name of God, thinking that they were justified.

Next I present a few cases from the life of Moses that inflicted fear in his heart and a misunderstanding of God's love, which also inspired millions who read them.

One of the cases is Moses' first encounter with God at the burning bush. This particular case is found in Exodus 4:1–17. The Lord is sending Moses to get the people out of Egypt. Moses feels that the job is too much for him, even impossible, and is trying to find excuses so that he can bail himself out. He even tells the Lord to send somebody else (verse 13). The following verse says that "the anger of the Lord was kindled against Moses" (verse 14). Kindled? How can a God like Jesus, who is, "merciful and gracious, longsuffering and abundant in goodness and truth," a God who is love, not control His anger in front of a shaking leaf like Moses? Didn't Jesus say, "learn of Me: for I am lowly in heart: and ye shall find rest unto your souls" (Matt. 11:29)? If Jesus was in the burning bush, talking with Moses, then the anger Moses felt most certainly did not come from the Lord but from someone who also was certainly there and trying desperately to confuse Moses about the great love God has for his people. Moses wrote this account based on what he felt while he was talking with God and thought the anger was coming from the Lord. Through Moses' mission, God was showing His love and mercy for His people, and Satan, even though invisible to Moses, was trying to pervert it. Instead of drawing near to God, Satan was inspiring Moses to run away from God, to fear Him. Jesus is the answer to all this confusion. All we need to do is compare Exodus 4:14 with the character of Jesus who never changes, and all becomes clear. Hebrews 13:8 reads, "Jesus Christ the same yesterday, and to day, and for ever."

Another case similar to this is found in the same chapter, Exodus 4:24-26. So we read verse 24: "And it came to pass by the way in the inn, that the Lord met him, and sought to kill him." How can the Lord send him on a mission and then, without warning or explanation, try to kill him? We know that Moses avoided a very sacred commandment to fulfill and that was to circumcise his son on the eighth day. We know that Moses was guilty because of that, but

God does not act like that. He will never turn against His servant without warning or explanation. Why would He try to kill Moses and at the same time inspire his wife, Zipporah, to quickly cut the foreskin of her son to save Moses' life? It makes no sense. Because Moses was guilty, Satan tried to kill him so that he could stop the deliverance of God's people from Egypt. God, being fully aware of Satan's plan, inspired Zipporah to fulfill what Moses avoided, and Moses could be thus justified, forgiven, and, of course, protected.

I present one last case about Moses, which is found in Numbers 14:1–38. The reader will have to read the entire context while I explain only the main points.

In chapter 13, Moses sent twelve spies to search the land of Canaan. The Lord delivered them from Egypt, He gave them the moral law and the ceremonial law at Mount Sinai, and now they were ready to receive the long-awaited promise, the land of Canaan.

So the twelve spies came back with their report; ten of them gave a discouraging report, while Joshua and Caleb gave a very encouraging report. All twelve spies agreed that the land was like a paradise, just like God promised. But the ten spies said that the people of the land were like giants compared to them. Therefore, humanly speaking, it was impossible to conquer the land. Joshua and Caleb were convinced that their God, who delivered them from Egypt performing great and powerful miracles, would do the same with the Canaanites, and no matter how tall and powerful those people seemed, they would be nothing to God. The entire congregation believed the bad report given by the ten spies and were all discouraged. They even thought to go back to Egypt, where they could remain slaves after such a spectacular deliverance. Joshua and Caleb tried to persuade them when they were actually talking to stone them. The appearance of the glory of the Lord in the tabernacle put an end to their cruel plan. The Lord had a conversation with Moses and planned to kill His rebellious people. Moses interceded for the people, kindly asking for forgiveness on their part and reminding the Lord of His reputation in case He decided to destroy His own people. Then He added, "And now, I beseech thee, let the power of my Lord be great, according as thou hast spoken, saying, The Lord is longsuffering, and of great mercy, forgiving iniquity and transgression" (vs. 17, 18). And the Lord answers in verse 20, "I have pardoned according to thy word."

Verse 20 is a key to the rest of the context. Please pay attention to the following verses. The Lord forgives and tells them to head back in the desert, "by the way of the Red Sea." If they don't want to go to Canaan, then the Lord won't force them to go there. From verse 26 to 35, the Lord presents them His final decision that they will roam in the desert for forty years and that all those who refused to conquer Canaan will die in the desert; only their children will inherit Canaan and, of course, Joshua and Caleb.

In the following verses from 36 to 38 we see something shocking in God's character. In our key verse, verse 20, we read that the Lord forgave the entire congregation without any exception. Moses mediated for pardon on behalf of his people in verse 19. If the Lord pardoned like He said, then why did He use a plague to kill those ten spies who brought an evil report? That does not match Jesus's character. He cannot forgive and still punish with such a terrible death. It sounds like God is taking vengeance on ten little worms. It is not God who killed the ten spies but Satan. Moses wrote what he thought happened, but he didn't know what really happened. God rejected those men, and Satan took control of this opportunity to inflict fear in everyone's hearts by killing those men with such a terrible death.

The great question that arises is: Why does God allow Satan to inflict fear in the hearts of all people and bring injustice to God's character? God is allowing Satan to show who he truly is. God is letting him even use His name and even play God to display his true character, but through Jesus to have him fully exposed (Ezekiel 28:17). Adam chose to eat of the Tree of Knowledge of Good and Evil. He made that decision for all of us unfortunately. Since then, everything on this planet is made up of good and evil. There is a time to laugh, and there is a time to cry; there is a time to build, and there is a time to destroy; we are born and we die; we eat many good things, but if we eat too much, it is bad for us; we need salt, which is good, but too much is bad; our bodies are good, but we also have a lot of bacteria within us; the air that we breathe is good, but it's also made up of other chemicals and pathogens that are bad for us; even the Bible, the very Word of God, is made up of good things and bad things. In some places it is clear as day, and other places are as dark as the night. Adam decided for all of us. That's why God gave us wisdom and grace to distinguish between good and evil, between God and Satan.

Jesus fasted for forty days in the wilderness, and at the end, when He was hungry, He heard a voice whispering to Him, "If thou be the Son of God, command that these stones be made bread" (Matt. 4:3). Right there and then, He had to distinguish based on the knowledge He acquired from the scriptures if this voice was from God or not. We know that He succeeded. We can succeed too with correct knowledge of God's character from scriptures and a loving, personal relationship with Him. This is what I am trying to present to you, the ability to distinguish God from millions of persons.

The spirit of Elijah is not fully aware of God's love but surely loves God by obeying Him in His Word. Jesus received from John the Baptist the spirit of Elijah through baptism, a spirit of obedience and love for God. He also received the Spirit of God, which taught Him the true love of God. This way He developed a balanced spirit of obedience and love toward God and a spirit of love toward humankind—especially enemies—taught from the heart of God.

The spirit of Elijah is the spirit of the Old Testament, which seeks vengeance because it was being inspired all the time by Moses. The Holy Spirit from the New Testament teaches to love even enemies, never seeking revenge because it has full knowledge of the love of God taught from Jesus.

Additions to Elisha's Case

There are more misunderstandings in Elisha's case that need to be brought to light. One of them is the encounter between Naaman the Syrian and Elisha. This account is found in 2 Kings chapter 5. In it is described the miraculous healing of Naaman, a pagan, from leprosy. One needs to read the entire chapter to become acquainted with the facts and to pay close attention to the words as we will analyze them carefully.

So Naaman is miraculously healed by God through His prophet Elisha. Then Gehazi, Elisha's disciple, thinks that he should benefit something from this rich man on behalf of his healing, which didn't cost him anything. Gehazi thought that his master, Elisha, was wrong for not asking anything in return for Naaman's healing and decides to go after him to ask for something Naaman had plenty of anyway. Naaman happily gave Gehazi double what he asked for, and Gehazi returned to Elisha. Little did Gehazi know that his master knew everything about what he just did because Elisha saw it in a vision. When Elisha asked him where he was, Gehazi lied to him because he knew that what he did with Naaman was wrong. In return, Elisha pronounced a curse upon him that "Naaman's leprosy shall cleave" unto him and to his seed "for ever" (v. 27).

If everything had remained the way it has been related until now, this passage would have been very easy to understand, and there would be no confusion and misunderstandings. Gehazi sinned,

Elisha cursed him in the name of the Lord, and God punished him with leprosy that, according to the words of Elisha, will never be healed. Therefore,he will die by the plague. But unfortunately, there's another passage that stands as a stumbling block to the curse that Elisha pronounced upon Gehazi, and that passage is found in 2 Kings 8:1–5. In this context, we see Gehazi talking to the king at least seven years later, if not more. Not only is he alive, but he certainly must have been healed; he would not be able to get close to the king if he had leprosy. Who healed him? Certainly not Elisha. Elisha told Gehazi that he'll die from leprosy, yet we see that the Lord endured him and healed him. This means that the curse did not come from God but from Elisha. Elisha pronounced it from himself. I'm not trying to say that Elisha is a false prophet but that the curse was neither pronounced nor approved by God.

If not God, then who brought the leprosy upon Gehazi? Do you see how quick Satan is in seeking opportunities? How quickly he brought confusion into the mind of Elisha and in the eyes of all who heard of and read this account.

Elisha has been rebuked before, when he resurrected the Shunammite's son (2 Kings 4:17–37). When he heard of his death, he sent Gehazi to run before him and to "lay his staff upon the face of the child." To the surprise of the prophet, nothing happened; the child was still dead. He went in the child's room and prayed this time. And after he prayed, he laid on top of the child and received a sign that God listened to his prayer by the warming of the child's body. He persisted this way, and only then did God resurrect the child. This was a lesson for Elisha that God is not a celestial room service that you call on by ringing a bell and to which He is supposed to answer promptly. No, he had to insist until he realized that God, and God alone, can make such a miracle. Man should never even think that just because he received gifts from God that from now on, man is the master of those gifts. The power still comes from God through those gifts.

Just so you understand what kind of confusion existed among

God's prophets in Israel, I want you to pay attention to this next account. It is found in 1 Kings 20:30–43. King Ahab overcomes the Syrian King Benhadad, and he lets him go despite God's commandment to kill him. In response to King Ahab's disobedience, the Lord sends a message to one of the sons of the prophets. The "sons of the prophets" was a group of young men who were not literally sons of prophets but indeed prophets. That was just a title they used. So this young man, after receiving the message from God, goes "unto his neighbor," not another prophet but someone close by, and demanded of him to hit him. This man refused to hit him, and as a consequence for "disobeying the voice of the Lord," the young man tells him that a lion will meet him and kill him. His word is fulfilled, and the man who refused to hit the prophet for no reason was killed by a lion (v. 36).

Is this the kind of God we serve? The prophet didn't even tell the man about his plan; he just told the man to hit him for no reason. How can God give such a commandment? And then, as a consequence for disobeying an unreasonable command, God kills him? To me, this young prophet sounds like Elisha and Elijah. Through his words, he told his neighbor something like this: "Because you have not obeyed my voice, which is like the voice of God, because I'm a prophet, you will be killed in a miraculous way. But it will be too late for you to realize it. Don't you know who I am? Well, now you'll know."

Why do you think that there was so much confusion and pride even among God's prophets? First of all, there was too much idolatry in Israel. But this shouldn't have been enough to cause that. There is no evidence that any of these prophets ever went to visit the temple in Jerusalem. It was mandatory for all men to go at least three times a year. No one could stand straight and walk upright without it. Jesus knew that He had to visit the temple and He did. Elijah didn't, and neither did Elisha or any of their followers. I think this was the biggest problem. No one is exempt from obedience to God's Word. Therefore, let us watch and pray so that we don't fall like them.

The Case of Abraham

In Genesis 22 we have one of the most amazing accounts written in the Bible. It portrays the love of God and the love of Abraham toward God, an account that sealed Abraham's fate as the father of all believers and the forefather of the Messiah. This account plays also as a prophesy about the death of Christ as a ransom for all people. Everyone has heard of the sacrifice of Abraham of his son, Isaac. It has been preached everywhere and explained millions of times, and yet there's something that has been missed because God's character, all along, hasn't been fully understood. So please pay close attention to what you're about to discover because it will help set the foundation to understanding His never-changing character, a foundation we have already started to build since the beginning of this book.

The chapter begins with God planning to tempt Abraham. "And he said, Take now thy son, thine only son Isaac, whom thou lovest, and get thee into the land of Moriah; and offer him there for a burnt offering upon one of the mountains which I will tell thee of."

There is no doubt that God is literally tempting Abraham. What is meant by tempting? To tempt someone means to persuade that someone to commit a sin or to transgress God's law. Can God tempt anybody, especially His people? Doesn't He know who Abraham is? He knows if Abraham is faithful. There is a verse that should clarify this dilemma beyond any doubt, and that verse is found in James

1:13: "Let no man say when he is tempted, I am tempted of God: for God cannot be tempted with evil, neither tempteth he any man." I think we should be clear that since God cannot tempt anyone, then He definitely did not tempt Abraham to kill his son for Him. It is against His own law. In Leviticus 18:21, 20:3, and Deuteronomy 12:30–31, 18:10, the Torah contains a number of imprecations against and laws forbidding child sacrifice and human sacrifice in general. The Tanakh denounces human sacrifices as barbaric customs of Baal worshippers (Psalm 106:37). How can God ask for that? The Lord tells Jeremiah regarding the same issue in Jeremiah 19:5: "They have built also the high places of Baal, to burn their sons with fire for burnt offerings unto Baal, which I commanded not, nor spake it, neither came it into my mind." Can we grasp this statement that says it never crossed God's mind to ask anyone for a human sacrifice, not even from Abraham?

Abraham's test was not about seeing if Abraham would kill his son but if he loved Isaac more than he loved God. Even the angel of the Lord tells him, "for now I know that thou fearest God, seeing thou hast not withheld thy son, thine only son for me" (v. 12). The biggest challenge of this context that someone may encounter is in verse 18 because it says, "And in thy seed shall all the nations of the earth be blessed; because thou hast obeyed my voice." Reading this verse makes one believe that God actually tempted Abraham, therefore transgressing His law. But what about the errors that Moses wrote? Weren't they considered God's voice, His words, His commandments? So is the case with Abraham. God allowed Satan to tempt Abraham, and because He allowed it, He considered it like His voice. The Lord took it upon Himself; if He allowed it, then He was responsible for it. Abraham did not have the written Word, so he could not have been tested on it. He was only tested on his priorities, whether God was his priority before Isaac. Satan will always ask to tempt God's people, and most of the time, God will allow it.

I know that for some people, this will be very hard to grasp. But for me, it is a risk worth taking to prove God's righteousness. If I'm wrong, then may the Lord have mercy on me the same way He had with Moses, Elijah, Elisha, and many others as we will continue to show throughout the rest of the book.

The Case of Job

The book of Job describes the most amazing account in the Bible and clearly unmasks the work of the devil, comparing his character with the ever-loving character of God. The book clearly points out who the real author of evil is. It also teaches that what happened in the life of Job happens in the lives of every believer. Whenever a person decides to live a godly life in Christ, Satan will always request to tempt that person, trying to prove that he or she does not deserve the grace of God because the individual is his servant.

A good example is Luke 22:31, 32, where the Lord tells Peter that Satan has asked to "sift" the disciples like wheat, meaning to try them. Verse 32 shows that his request was taken very seriously. The Lord tells Peter that instead of denying Satan's request, they should be prepared to prove Satan wrong. The Lord came to snatch us from the claws of Satan; we were Satan's servants. He is telling the devil that his servants don't want to serve him anymore. The devil is never convinced; that's why he will try to prove they are all wrong. We all have to prove him wrong. James tells us in James 4:7, "Submit yourselves therefore to God. Resist the devil, and he will flee from you."

The book starts with a dialogue between God and Satan, where God is praising his servant Job as a "perfect and an upright man" as there was none like him on the earth (Job 2:3). Satan replies that the reason that Job served God was because God bribed him with many blessings. So Satan asked to prove God wrong, saying that if the blessings would be retracted, Job wouldn't be God's servant anymore, but Satan's, cursing God "to his face."

So the first trial is permitted with only one interdiction, that Satan should not touch him. Job passes the first trial with success, humiliating Satan. God proved to Satan and to the whole universe that He is still omniscient, but Satan is not giving up. He argues that the interdiction worked on God's behalf, and that's why he couldn't succeed. If God lifted the interdiction, the whole universe would be a witness to a different outcome. So the second trial is permitted, the sanction is lifted, and Satan is now allowed to do anything he can imagine to prove God wrong. A new interdiction, which is a logical one, has replaced the first one, where Satan cannot kill Job, because by killing him, he wouldn't prove anything. And God can raise him from the dead because He is not done with His servant.

So Satan hits the innocent Job with a terrible disease. Even though in great pain, Job still praises God. So far, Satan's trial failed, but the devil is still not convinced. He inspires Job's wife to persuade him to curse God and die, but Job can't be sold (Job 2:9, 10). Then Satan brings in his best friends, who desperately try to convince Job that this suffering is from God because the Lord must be angry with him. Job must have sinned somehow, and God is making him pay. Let us not forget that nobody knew what was actually happening. Everybody was convinced that Job's suffering was God's judgment. Job is the only one who doesn't know why God is angry with him. He tells his friends that he never sinned; at least he cannot recall any sin in his life. That's why this apparent punishment does not make sense to him. Job's friends, however, still insist that there must be a sin. They have become so desperate that they accuse him of sending, "the widows away empty," and breaking, "the arms of the fatherless" (Job 22:9). Here they knew they were lying.

One of the reasons they were so desperate in convincing him that he sinned is that one of them, Eliphaz, had a vision from Satan pretending to be an angel of light (Job 4:12–21). During that encounter, Satan was trying to convince Eliphaz that all men, including Job, are sinners. Satan's statements have convinced Eliphaz that this angel was sent by God to enlighten him regarding Job's suffering. With this, Eliphaz was convinced that God was against Job.

During his suffering, Job manifested his faith in the first coming of the Messiah and also in the second (Job 19:23–29). His friends mentioned nothing about it but continued to agonize him with their accusations.

Then something strange happened starting with chapter 38 and continuing until chapter 42. A whirlwind starts, and the "Lord" anxiously, as if He couldn't take it anymore, starts to speak, "out of the whirlwind." According to His words, it seems like He is taking sides with Job's friends, who haven't been very friendly with him. He starts with these words: "Who is this that darkeneth counsel by words without knowledge?" talking about Job (38:2). Then He continues by challenging Job with questions inspired from the character of a bully. It's as if the "Lord "is trying to put His fists up to start a one-on-one match with Job, demanding him to show what he's got. It seems as if the "Lord "is infuriated over the fact that Job pretends that he never sinned, being perfect like God is, which was also taught by Jesus (Matt. 5:48). Didn't God declare him perfect from the beginning of the book? Why is He now angry that Job is pretending to be exactly what God said he was? Did God change, or did something else happen? When God told Satan not to kill Job, God actually put only one interdiction upon Satan. He pretty much told him that he can do anything he can think of to make Job curse God, except kill him. He can even play God if that would help the devil reach his goal. God gave him freedom to exercise his wisdom and power in any way possible so that he can prove God wrong.

In a previous study, we discovered that in 1 Kings 19:9–13, the Lord showed Elijah how He speaks and behaves. And one of the ways that God does not like to behave and to speak from is, "a strong wind." He will not be present in a strong wind, like the whirlwind in question. During the Lord's speech, not one word was mentioned about the first or the second coming of the Messiah. In fact, He asked Job if He can, "tread down the wicked in their place" (Job 40:12). Is that what the Lord is about, to tread the wicked or to save them? Why didn't He ask Job if he could save them by dying in their place? God also accused him of nullifying His judgment and condemning Him by upholding his righteousness (Job 40:8). Yet at the end, God is praising Job for speaking righteously about Him and accusing Job's friends of speaking unjustly about Him after "the Lord" took their side against Job (Job 42:7).

The whole thing just does not make sense. If the Lord was speaking from chapter 38 to 41, then the Lord has a changing character, thus denying His Word. Therefore, He cannot be trusted. I do not see Jesus in that character. That's why it would make the most perfect sense if we agree that the person speaking in those chapters could only be Satan, trying desperately to make Job curse or deny God. We can clearly see that the character of the person speaking in chapter 42 is different than the character in the previous chapters. I hope and pray that this descriptive account makes as much sense to you as it does to me.

The Case of Samuel

Prophet Samuel is well known for his piety and love for God and His people. He didn't just occupy the office of a judge and a prophet, he served God and His people out of pure love. Even though he was the last judge, he was like another Moses. Through him the time of the judges ended, and the time of the kings began. The way the line of kings had started is a bit confusing and misunderstood, and it needs to be given careful attention.

The first king who was anointed was Saul. The reason he was chosen was because the people got tired of being different from the other nations and wanted to be in the same fashion as they; they wanted a king. They forgot that their king was the Lord, and they actually got tired of Him. Doing so, they weren't just rejecting Samuel as a judge, but they were rejecting God as their King (1 Sam. 8:4–7).

One day Saul lost his donkeys and went to ask prophet Samuel for help finding them. The day before Saul went to Samuel, "the Lord had told Samuel in his ear a day before Saul came, saying, To morrow about this time I will send thee a man out of the land of Benjamin, and thou shalt anoint him to be captain over my people Israel, that he may save my people out of the hand of the Philistines: for I have looked upon my people, because their cry is come unto me" (1 Sam. 9:15, 16). Who do you think is talking to Samuel here?

A careful study of this passage will prove to have a few major discrepancies. The first discrepancy is that the "Lord" is choosing a king from the tribe of Benjamin. As prophesied by Jacob the patriarch, the line of kings was supposed to come from the tribe of Judah: "The sceptre shall not depart from Judah, nor a lawgiver from between his feet, until Shiloh come; and unto him shall the gathering of the people be" (Gen. 49:10). Here is enough proof that the tribe the line of kings was supposed to come from, including the Messiah, was the tribe of Judah, not Benjamin. Here the "Lord" has transgressed His own prophetic word.

The second discrepancy is, "that he may save my people out of the hand of the Philistines." Let the reader not forget that when Saul died, he left Israel in bondage to the Philistines (1 Sam. 31:7). When the Lord prophesied that Samson would deliver Israel out of the hands of the Philistines (Judg. 13:5), it was fulfilled precisely (Judg. 16:30). This prophesy concerning Saul was not fulfilled.

The third discrepancy is "because their cry is come unto me." Let's not forget that weeks or months before, Israel had rejected the Lord to be their king by asking for a king, and the Lord has confirmed that to Samuel (1 Sam. 8:7). When His people sin against God, they put a wall between them and Him. And that means our prayers cannot reach Him until His people repent (Isa. 59:1, 2). In our context, there is no evidence that His people repented of that evil choice, which means their cries did not pass that wall. Therefore they did not reach the real Lord.

Do you see what is going on? Can you see how dangerous the consequences of disobedience are? The same thing that happened in the time of Moses has happened again in the time of Samuel. If the people choose to disobey God, that automatically means they chose to obey Satan; and God will allow it. God allows our choices the same way He allowed the choice of Adam and Eve. God doesn't force obedience. Did this make Samuel a bad prophet? No, for the same reason that Moses was not a bad teacher. They spoke and taught what God intentionally allowed because of the hardening of the people, not the prophets. This should be a warning to all of us. Beware and obey!

There are some things we should know about Samuel that will help us understand why God allowed Saul to be anointed as king. Through these things we see God's righteousness in His dealings with Samuel.

Samuel is born into a polygamist family (1 Sam. 1:1, 2). This was not a spiritually healthy atmosphere for any child. Then the child Samuel was brought to Eli, the priest, to be consecrated to the Lord. Eli was not a good teacher. His sons grew up to be very immoral (1 Sam. 2:12–17). Everybody in Israel knew that, including Hannah, the mother of Samuel. It wasn't very wise of her to place her son in the hands of such an incapable man to raise children properly. You did not have to give your child to the priests in order to consecrate him or her to the Lord. Samson had been consecrated to the Lord by the Lord Himself, and his parents were not told that they should give their child to anyone, rather, they could raise him themselves (Judg. 13:1–14). This is what led Samuel to raise his sons to be almost like Eli's sons (1 Sam. 8:1–5). We can see from the context that the people had enough of them, using that as an excuse to anoint a king over them.

Then we see Samuel working as a priest. This is actually a big problem because he was not born from the bloodline of Aaron. I'm sure that many do not know that Samuel was a Levite (1 Chron. 6:27, 28, 33, 34). According to the Law, he was not allowed to bring any sacrifices. He got very angry at Saul one time, when he dared to bring a sacrifice. But what about him? Wasn't God angry with him because he wasn't a real priest (1 Sam. 13:9–14)? I think so, but the Lord didn't make it public. The Lord is not going to change His Law to make Samuel fit in it.

The problem was not only that he wasn't allowed to bring sacrifices, but he brings them on high places (1 Sam. 9:12). This was clearly forbidden by the Law (Lev. 17: 3, 4; Deut. 12:4–6, 11, 13, 14; Ex. 20:26). Somehow, Samuel must've missed it or blatantly disobeyed it when he read it. That means he didn't study the Law very carefully.

Therefore, it should not be surprising that God allowed the devil to use Samuel in such a way, contrary to His teachings. It was only after Samuel is fired from his position as a judge and a priest, when Saul is anointed in his place, that God is able to use him correctly by anointing David as king in Saul's place. From that point on, he was in accordance with the Law.

We will present one last case about Samuel's character manifested in his behavior in 1 Samuel 15:32, 33. In this context, Samuel goes to Saul to rebuke him for disobeying God's commandment in keeping Agab, the king of Amalekites, alive and for keeping the best of all the animals. In this situation, Samuel, "hewed Agab in pieces before the Lord in Gilgal." He didn't just kill him but cut him in pieces. Was that his job to do? No! That was Saul's job. How can a priest, a prophet, and a judge do something like that? He definitely lost control here.

This should be an eye-opener to everyone about what it means to disobey God's Word. The consequences are colossal; he even says that (1 Sam. 15:22, 23). God never forgot Samuel nor forsook him because he was indeed consecrated unto Him. God worked with what He had. God is love, but He is also just. He will not change for anyone, not even for Jesus. Jesus was the Son of God, but that did not exempt Him from obedience. His strict obedience is what made Him the Savior of the world.

The Case of Uzzah

The case of Uzzah is another one that deserves careful attention. It is found in 2 Samuel 6:1–11 and 1 Chronicles 13:1–14. If studied carefully, we'll be able to see God's fairness in this account.

King David was established in Jerusalem, naming it the city of David. He decided that the ark of the covenant should dwell with him in his city so he can have God closer to him. They decided to set the ark upon a new cart that was pulled by oxen. On the way to Jerusalem, there was great joy, with singing and dancing. The cart was going a little too fast, and the ark was being shaken to the point that it was going to fall. To prevent it from falling, Uzzah tried to grab it because he was next to it on the cart. The moment he touched it, the Bible says that "the anger of the Lord was kindled against Uzzah; and God smote him there for his error; and there he died by the ark of God" (2 Sam. 6:6, 7).

We need to get this straight about the long-suffering of God. Everybody was happy that the ark of God, which is His throne, was being moved to the capital of Israel, giving it the greatest honor. On its way there, the ark was about to fall, and instead of preventing it from falling, the Lord would have been more pleased to see it fall and maybe even damaged. But no! The long-suffering of God couldn't endure to see His throne being saved from damage and mockery that it chose to kill the one who dared to spare God's throne. We know that according to the law of Moses, only the Levites were allowed to carry the ark manually and not by cart. But Uzzah and all the people neglected to study, and Uzzah was killed without warning. Why wasn't Saul killed when he brought a sacrifice he knew he wasn't allowed to do so (1 Sam. 13:8–13)? Why wasn't King David killed when he sinned with Bathsheba and killed Uriah knowing that it was wrong? Why wasn't Solomon killed when he filled Jerusalem with temples dedicated to idols, even though he knew it was wrong? Why wasn't Judas killed the moment he sold Jesus for thirty pieces of silver? Why wasn't Peter killed when he denied Jesus three times? I can go on and on. Why wasn't God's anger kindled then? Uzzah and all the others didn't know that what they were doing was wrong. I think it's obvious that Satan saw an opportunity, and he took advantage of it. The Lord could not have part of what His people were doing because they acted neglectfully, but He allowed Satan to act according to his own will, and at the same time under God's full control, so that His people could learn not to play with fire again. God allowing Satan to kill Uzzah taught His people to study. As a matter of fact, in 1 Chronicles 15:12, 13, David, speaking to the Levites after the death of Uzzah, when he decided to bring the ark again to Jerusalem, said, "Ye are the chief fathers of the Levites: sanctify yourselves, both ye and your brethren, that ye may bring up the ark of the Lord God of Israel unto the place that I have prepared for it. For because ye did it not at first, the Lord our God made a breach upon us, for that we sought him not after the due order," or according to the ceremonial law. So God knew why He allowed Satan to kill Uzzah; the devil didn't even know that he was actually promoting God's work.

The Case of King Josiah

Paying attention to the words and the language of a text is crucial in Bible interpretation. Certain verses contain important definitions of specific words or symbols, to the point where they become laws of interpretation for those words or symbols considered in similar cases. The case of King Josiah is unique in this application, proving that what God has once said will not change. So let's study this account found in 2 Chronicles 34:20–28 and 35:20–24.

King Josiah is, by far, the biggest reformer in the Davidic dynasty. He and his work have been prophesied since the reign of King Jeroboam by exact name and the kind of work that he did (1 Kings 13:1–5). The feast of Passover celebrated in his days hadn't been celebrated in such a way, "in Israel from the days of Samuel the prophet; neither did all the kings of Israel keep such a Passover as Josiah kept" (2 Chron. 35:18). He even surpassed King David.

One time the priest Hilkiah found a book of the Law. The priests read it in the presence of the king, and the king was deeply moved. He set it in his heart to follow everything that was written in it. In doing so, he thought to ask the Word of God through a prophet. He sent his representatives to a prophetess named Huldah, the wife of Shallum. She praised the king's zeal that he showed for the Word of God, and in the end, this is what she told him: "Behold, I will gather thee to thy fathers, and thou shalt be gathered to thy grave in peace" (2 Chron. 34:28). If we continue to read chapter 35, from verses 20 to 24, we will see that Josiah did not die in peace. Rather, he died in rebellion and war. King Necho warned him not to fight with him, and his words were the very words of God. Necho was telling Josiah what God commanded him, and Josiah didn't listen. He went to war with Necho and killed him. So in conclusion, the words of Huldah were not fulfilled. Her words inspired him to disobedience and rebellion.

In Deuteronomy 18:21 and 22, Moses taught how to distinguish between true and false prophets. If the words of that prophet are not fulfilled, "that is the thing which the Lord hath not spoken, but the prophet hath spoken it presumptuously." According to this teaching of Moses, Huldah must be a false prophet. And why shouldn't she be? Paul teaches us in 1 Corinthians 14:34–37 that the Lord's commandment is that women are not called to be prophets or teachers. The same is found in 1 Timothy 2:11–14. What exactly this means is that a woman is not allowed to occupy the office of a prophet. For example, David prophesied, but he never occupied the position of a prophet. When he needed to ask God for guidance, he had to ask his prophets Nathan or Gad, or the high priest. King Saul prophesied, but he was not an official prophet (1 Sam. 10:10–12). He also had to ask God through Samuel, who occupied the position of a prophet. Isaiah occupied the position of a prophet, Jeremiah, Ezekiel, Moses, and so on. There have been women who prophesied but were never prophets. Among them are Hannah (1 Sam. 2:1–10); Miriam, the sister of Moses (Num. 12:1, 2); Elisabeth, the mother of John the Baptist (Luke 1:41–45); and Mary, the mother of Jesus (Luke 1:46–55). Yet there is only one woman who actually occupied the position of a prophet, and that was Deborah (Judg. 4 and 5). The reason she was chosen as a prophet was because men in her time had become cowards (Judg. 5:7). Her election as a prophet was like a slap in the face to all men. And it was. Ever since then, God has chosen men to be prophets.

The Case of Ezekiel

We present one last case in the Old Testament to prove God's unchanging love and character that has been misunderstood for centuries. This one is found in the book of Ezekiel, chapter 21, verses 1 through 17. Here the Lord says that He will cut off from the land of Israel, "the righteous and the wicked" (vs. 3, 4). How can this be? On one event in Genesis 18:24, 25, Abraham pleaded with the Lord for the wicked people of Sodom and Gomorrah, and this is what he said, "Peradventure there be fifty righteous within the city: wilt thou also destroy and not spare the place for the fifty righteous that are therein? That be far from thee to do after this manner, to slay the righteous with the wicked: and that the righteous should be as the wicked, that be far from thee: Shall not the Judge of all the earth do right?" And what did the Lord answer him? "If I find in Sodom fifty righteous within the city, then I will spare all the place for their sakes" (vs. 26), meaning that killing the righteous with the wicked would be unjust. Then when did God change?

The dialogue goes on between God and Ezekiel. In verse 14, God tells Ezekiel to prophesy a slaughter for Jerusalem and his people, and to "smite his hands together," meaning to clap for joy because of the slaughter prophesied as a revenge of the Lord. In verse 17, the Lord says, "I will also smite mine hands together (clap for joy), and I will cause my fury to rest: I the Lord have said it". Really? In other words, God will find pleasure in seeing His people slaughtered? He will be happy to take revenge on His children? That is a new one for me! All along I thought that God was love, never finding pleasure in the death of the wicked (Ezek. 18:23, 32; 33:11). Here the devil is tempting Ezekiel by inflicting fear in his heart regarding God's character. The devil wants to portray God as a tyrant, and this he succeeded in doing. That's why we need the Holy Spirit to be able to discern the truth.

THE CASES OF
THE NEW TESTAMENT

The Case of the New Church

We have shown a lot of misunderstandings about God's love and long-suffering in the Old Testament. But what about in the New Testament? If God allowed Satan to inflict fear and confusion before Christ's birth, did that continue after? Let's take a look and analyze together so that we can get a better understanding of God's love and long-suffering that surpasses our limited understanding.

Before He ascended to heaven, Jesus instructed His apostles, "that they should not depart from Jerusalem, but wait for the promise of the Father, which, saith he, ye have heard of me. For John truly baptized with water; but ye shall be baptized with the Holy Ghost not many days hence." And then He continues, "But ye shall receive power, after that the Holy Ghost is come upon you: and ye shall be witnesses unto me both in Jerusalem, and in all Judea, and in Samaria, and unto the uttermost part of the earth" (Acts 1:4, 5, 8). What Jesus meant here is that they should have waited in Jerusalem until they received the Holy Spirit, and then they should have gone to the whole world. Did they obey His command? Let's analyze.

If we read the book of Acts, we see that immediately after they received the Holy Spirit, they remained in Jerusalem, developing a socialist system of affairs, and this can be proven. In Acts 2:44–47 and 4:32–37, we read that those who had "possessions and goods" sold them and gave them to the church, "and had all things common." Nobody was working anymore, not even the apostles.

All the resources wouldn't have lasted forever. If this was the way Jesus prescribed, then why did He allow a persecution to come upon the church through the death of Stephen, putting an end to this socialist system to never be adopted again until the papacy incorporated it within the Catholic Church? If the Lord hadn't put an end to this socialist system early enough, the church would not have been what it is today, or it would have ceased to exist. If that socialist system was the way of the future for the church, then why do we see Paul teaching all that are spreading the gospel to work with their hands, using himself as an example (Acts 20:33–35)? Even Jesus said, "freely ye have received, freely give" (Matt. 10:8). Therefore, receiving wages for spreading the gospel would be a sin. If everyone sold their possessions, then they became dependent on the church. They couldn't even leave the church if they wanted to; they were stuck depending on the church. The Lord never intended that for the church. Everyone has to depend on Him and still keep their independence.

Let's continue with our analysis because there's more, and it gets even worse. In Acts 5:1–11, we read a very powerful account about Ananias and Sapphira, who sold a possession, "and kept back part of the price." The part of the price that they didn't keep they brought to the church, telling everyone they brought the whole price. Peter felt that they were lying and unmasked them, saying that they lied "to the Holy Ghost." They both died instantly, first Ananias and then Sapphira. And at the end, it says that "great fear came upon all the church, and upon as many as heard these things" (v. 11).

We all have to agree that this couple sinned by embellishing their gift and charity before all. But still, they did what they wanted with their possession. Didn't Peter ask them that (v. 4)? They wanted to hide a part of it, and they did. It was not Peter's business to cry aloud that they lied to the church about their gift. He could've taken them aside and rebuked them privately, like Jesus advised us to do (Matt. 18:15–17). He didn't have to make a show out of it because the church was robbed of her income. In verse 8, Peter asks

Sapphira if they sold the land for "so much." What? That was none of his business, especially after he knew the truth from Ananias. He starts to sound like Elijah, kind of like, "Don't you know who I am?" Because he makes miracles, he thinks that God is allowing him to behave this way. The apostles were in danger of becoming dictators. After this incident, everybody was afraid of the apostles, and they probably made sure to bring more of their possessions to the church lest they be cursed. That sounds a lot like the system adopted by the papacy during the Dark Ages, where all those who did not listen to the papacy were cursed, fined, imprisoned, or put to death.

If we go back a little bit, in Acts 4 Peter and John are taken into custody by the Sanhedrin for healing a lame man. They give their testimony to the Sanhedrin, and then they are released. When they came back to the church, they all started praising God and praying for strength to continue preaching the gospel. Then verse 31 from chapter 4 says, "And when they had prayed, the place was shaken where they were assembled together; and they were all filled with the Holy Ghost, and they spake the word of God with boldness." First of all, we have proved in a previous study that God is not in earthquakes (1 Kings 19:11). Second, they are still in Jerusalem, never even thinking about the Great Commission to go to the rest of the world. This earthquake makes them feel even more comfortable continuing the work in Jerusalem. Did this earthquake remind them they have a responsibility that they forgot about? Of course not because God was not in the earthquake.

In both cases, Ananias and Sapphira and the earthquake, we can see that the church's disobedience and backsliding opened the door to Satan, who saw an opportunity and acted promptly to gain territory. Disobedience is as guilty as witchcraft (1 Sam. 15:22–23). Because of their disobedience, the devil encouraged the disciples to remain in Jerusalem, making them feel certain that the Lord was with them because the earthquake assured them so, and inflicting fear toward the church's organization so that he could maintain the socialist system within it. Can you imagine? To be afraid of God's church?

That is His plan? No, no, no! Never! Just because the Lord made a miracle with the lame man through Peter in chapter 3, they think that God was approving them. God can be with a person to promote His work but not necessarily approve his or her behavior. "Many will say to me in that day, Lord, Lord, have we not prophesied in thy name? and in thy name have cast out devils? and in thy name done many wonderful works? And then will I profess unto them, I never knew you: depart from me, ye that work iniquity" (Matt. 7:22, 23).

The Case of Paul

Paul is the most famous apostle by far because he worked the most and wrote the most. He was chosen in a unique way, unlike the others, and his conversion culminated from a general in Satan's army to a servant in the Lord's kingdom of heaven, the church. Even though an apostle, Paul was still a man chosen only to proclaim the gospel to the world. He still remained 100 percent human, and we will see that in this study. We will study his case a little bit differently. We look at the key objective presented by a question and then analyze it in detail to come up with the answer. It will be like a test to see if we understood everything we have gone over so far.

In the book of Acts, chapters 21 to 23, Paul has been arrested, and one night, "the Lord stood by him, and said, Be of good cheer, Paul: for as thou hast testified of me in Jerusalem, so must thou bear witness also at Rome" (23:11). And here is the shocking question: Who is really talking to Paul? Of course you're going to say that the verse says clearly, "the Lord." That was easy, but that is the easy way out. The Bible was not meant to be easy; it was meant to be studied. So let's study it. Let's analyze it deeply and squeeze the truth out of it. We will not try to rewrite the Bible but to make sense out of it.

In the book of Acts, Paul worked very effectively until his third trip. Every time he returned from his trips, he went first to Jerusalem and then back home to Antioch. The Lord told him from the beginning of his ministry to get out of Jerusalem because they—the

Jews—would not receive his testimony about Jesus (Acts 22:17–21). The Lord chose him for the Gentiles, and even Paul recognized this (Acts 13:46, 47; 18:6; Gal. 2:9). Then why is he always going to Jerusalem when the Lord commanded him to leave that place alone?

In Acts 18:18, Paul shaved his head according to the ceremonial law. Why? Didn't he preach that the ceremonial law ended at the cross (Eph. 2:14–16; Col. 2:14). In Acts 20:6, we see him celebrating the feast of unleavened bread. Why? In Acts 20:7–12 we see Paul exhausting the disciples with long sermons, "even till break of day." As a result of that long sermon, a disciple dies. But through God's grace, he was brought back to life.

In Tyre we see Paul make a great mistake, disobeying the voice of the Spirit that was warning him through the disciples not to go to Jerusalem (Acts 21:4–6). After he rejects the Spirit's warning, the fate of Paul is sealed through prophet Agabus (Acts 21:10, 11).

In Jerusalem, being brainwashed by the disciples there—especially by James, the Lord's brother—he makes another grave mistake by bringing sacrifices, against his own teachings (Acts 21:17–26). After he is arrested, Paul holds a sermon to some people the Lord had not sent him to, and they don't even want to listen to him (Acts 22:22, 23).

On his way to Jerusalem, Paul told everyone that he was ready to die for the Lord. But as they were getting ready to whip him, Paul saved himself by telling them he was a Roman citizen (Acts 20:24; 21:13; 22:24–29). Jesus did not do this.

When he is brought before the Sanhedrin, Paul mocked the high priest in revenge for the smacking he received. And when he was asked why he used such words to address the high priest, he felt rebuked and apologized, lying that he didn't know he was the high priest, when everybody knew who the high priest was (Acts 23:1–5). During the meeting of the Sanhedrin, Paul renamed himself a Pharisee and brother with the Pharisees, a title that he renounced after his baptism (Acts 23:6; Phil. 3:5–8). He caused confusion within the meeting of the Sanhedrin so that he might avoid suffering (Acts 23:6–9). Jesus didn't do anything like this, even though He could.

And now comes the key verse of our discussion: "And the night following the Lord stood by him, and said, Be of good cheer, Paul: for as thou hast testified of me in Jerusalem, so must thou bear witness also at Rome" (Acts 23:11).

What kind of testimony did Paul give in Jerusalem, I ask you? A good one? I don't see that. That's why I think it wasn't the Lord who spoke with him but Satan, who tried to deceive him by pretending to be the Lord. The devil knew from the prophecy of Agabus that God would not allow him to kill Paul in Jerusalem. And here Satan makes a plan to take him to Rome. He makes Paul ask to be taken to Rome. If we carefully study Paul's judgment by Governor Festus from Acts 25, we see that Paul, not the Lord, asked to be judged in Rome (Acts 25:10, 11; 28:18, 19). Paul feared that he was going to die unjustly in Jerusalem, while the Lord promised him through Agabus that he was only going to be tied. Even though the priests were planning to have him killed on his way to Jerusalem (Acts 25:2, 3), the Lord could've protected him and set him free (Acts 26:30–32). Therefore, the Lord had it in His plan to set him free. But because Paul believed the words of Satan to be the words of the Lord, he fell in a trap. In other words, what kind of judgment did the Cesar give him? A fair one? Didn't he die by the hand of the Cesar in whose safety he trusted? If he hadn't asked to be taken to Rome, he wouldn't have died in Jerusalem, and he would have been set free (Acts 28:17–19).

In conclusion, Paul needs to receive the respect that he deserves. He was 100 percent apostle, but he also was 100 percent human. When we study his writings, or the writings of all the prophets, we need to study them carefully because God did not eliminate the human factor. That's why Jesus is the only perfect example for us to follow.

The Case of the Eternal Fire

Out of all the cases that we discussed so far about God's love, no other subject brings more doubt about His great love and justice than the eternal fire. The thought of burning forever—for trillions and trillions of years—has either terrified millions who tried to approach an ever-loving God and gave up on Him, or has turned millions of so-called believers into hypocrites. The worst criminals ever convicted in human history have either been punished to death or imprisoned for life. Some have been tortured for different reasons, fair or unfair ones, but in the end, they died, and their suffering ceased. Can God be just in His judgment to give eternal punishment of the worst pain known to people equally to everyone who didn't fit His criteria, whether they have sinned a lot or a little? Can Ananias and Sapphira receive the same punishment equal in duration and pain as Hitler or Stalin? How about Satan? He is definitely the guiltiest of all the fallen creatures. Would you accept to share the same punishment with him? Or would you approve that all your loved ones who might not make it through the last judgment share the same punishment as Satan? Be honest with yourself, and judge as if your eternal life depended on it. Do not accept it and turn into a hypocrite, embracing God with cold, shaking hands, kissing Him with shivering lips, trembling and stuttering as you try to convince Him how much you really love Him for His awesome and amazing grace. Get real. Try to find another image of God unmarred of limited human innovation and interpretation, one that is fair and said that the unfaithful will receive different kinds of punishment (Luke 12:47, 48).

The context in question is found in the book of Revelation 14:9–11. Let me remind the reader that the book of Revelation is almost entirely symbolic, meaning that the symbols need to be interpreted correctly and not taken literally. In Revelation, we find symbols like beasts with four faces; dragons with seven heads; locusts with crowns of gold, faces of men, breastplates of iron; teeth like lions', and so on. Therefore, our passage in question is also written in symbolic sense because, as described above, it does not make sense literally. So if we can find the explanation of eternal fire in other passages of the Bible, then we will have the correct interpretation. We have to let the Bible and only the Bible explain itself. If the Bible cannot explain itself, then it is inconsistent and can't be trusted.

If we take a look at Isaiah chapter 34, we find a similar passage from verses 8 to 10. The passage refers to the country of Edom being punished by God. It says that the, "land thereof shall become burning pitch. It shall not be quenched night or day; the smoke thereof shall go up forever: from generation to generation it shall lie waste; none shall pass through it for ever and ever." Did the land of Edom ever become "burning pitch," whose smoke and fire would be seen even today? I don't think so, and neither do you. Not only is that not true, it is absurd. The population, and not the land of Edom, was destroyed by Nebuchadnezzar. The effect of that destruction was as if a fire passed through, destroying the population and its major cities, and the soil was so contaminated that no one would ever want to live there. Once destroyed by Nebuchadnezzar, the cities and the population of Edom were never to be renewed and rebuilt. When the Jews came back from the Babylonian captivity, their population was renewed and their cities rebuilt. This was not the case with Edom. The population and territory ceased to exist forever.

Another passage similar to the one in question is found in Jude verse 7: "Even as Sodom and Gomorrha, and the cities about them in like manner, giving themselves over to fornication, and going after strange flesh, are set forth for an example, suffering the vengeance of eternal fire." If these cities were literally suffering the vengeance of eternal fire, then we should be able to see that fire today. Where were those cities located? At the south of the Dead Sea. There is no Sodom and no Gomorra there anymore, and there is no more fire. So the interpretation has to be symbolic. The destruction of those cities was eternal. Those cities and their populations were never to be restored.

The same will happen at the end of time, when Jesus comes for the second time. He will destroy with fire all the unbelievers, including Satan and his fallen angels. It is possible that some will suffer the effects of that fire more than others according to their guilt. This remains to be decided by God. The one who will probably suffer most will be Satan.

From this destruction, there will be no more resurrection. This will be their everlasting destruction. Think about it. The reason for punishment is to make a person change for the better. Eternal fire or punishment doesn't give anyone a chance to change. There will be no forgiveness from it. There will be no way out of that torture. You can ask for forgiveness all you want, but you'll never see it. So guess what the unfaithful will do in that fire. They will curse God's name forever, which means that sin will be everlasting. Sin will live eternally as long as those sinners live eternally in that fire. So the wages of sin are not death but everlasting life in fire.

Wrong! Death means death (Romans 6:23). The literal translation of everlasting fire just doesn't make sense but contradicts the very Word and love of God.

Paying Close Attention to the Words Is Crucial

After the fall everything changed. The relationship between God and humankind was not the same. Therefore, the way that God was communicating to humanity was not going to be the same as it was before the fall. That's why I think paying close attention to the words of God is crucial in understanding His will and His love for us. Let me demonstrate that from the words of Jesus and of God.

One day the disciples came to Jesus and asked Him, "Why speakest thou unto them in parables?" (Matt. 13:10). He answered them that even though they hear, they should not understand, and even though they have eyes, they should not see, "lest at any time they should be converted, and their sins should be forgiven them" (Matt. 13:10–15; Mark 4:9–12; Luke 8:9, 10). A literal interpretation and a quick look will make us believe that Jesus is kind of harsh with humanity, or at least with part of it. But thinking about it will make us question ourselves: Why did He bother to come in human flesh and suffer for them if they are not supposed to see and hear the truth? It really makes no sense. It's just a figure of speech that is supposed to make us dig deep in His words and understand His intentions.

This passage is very similar in nature of speech to Genesis 3:22–24:

And the Lord God said, Behold, the man is become as one of us, to know good and evil: and now, lest he put forth his hand, and take also of the tree of life, and eat, and live forever: Therefore the Lord God sent him forth from the garden of Eden, to till the ground from whence he was taken. So he drove out the man; and he placed at the east of the garden of Eden Cherubims, and a flaming sword which turned every way, to keep the way of the tree of life.

Verse 22 seems to speak about humankind's interdiction from the Tree of Life. It seems as if the fruit of the tree had been able to give man eternal life while being a sinner, he could have lived forever if he ate from it. However, the language is symbolic. It is the same as Matthew 13:13–15, Mark 4:10–12, and John 12:39, 40. The key to a correct interpretation is found in Genesis 3:24. On the way to the Tree of Life, God placed cherubim and a sword. What do cherubim represent? In Ezekiel 1, we see a description of four living creatures that are called cherubim in chapter 10 verses 5–9, 15, 16, 19, 20, and 11:22. All four creatures have four faces—a face of a man, a face of a lion, a face of an ox, and a face of an eagle (Ezek. 1:10). We see a similar passage with four similar creatures in Revelation 4:6–11. They have the same faces as the ones in Ezekiel 1:10, which would make it safe to say that these are also cherubim.

What is special about these cherubim is that in chapter 5 of Revelation, we see them sing a special song, and this is what they say: "for thou wast slain, and hast redeemed us to God by thy blood out of every kindred, and tongue, and people, and nation; And hast made us unto our God kings and priests: and we shall reign on the earth" (v. 9, 10). They simply say that Jesus died for them and has made them kings and priests that will reign on earth. This means that these creatures are a symbol of human beings, people redeemed by Christ. Therefore, cherubim represent God's people.

The "flaming sword" that the Lord placed at the east of the

garden is a symbol of the Word of God (Eph. 6:17; Heb. 4:12; Rev. 2:16). So from these references, we can come up with a clear interpretation of the symbols that God used to create the picture described in Genesis 3:22–24, and this is it: The way to the Tree of Life is through the Word and God's people. That sword, "turned every way," means that it calls everyone from anywhere in the world. God doesn't want to stop anyone from coming to the Tree of Life. He's actually calling everyone. Through this picture, God wants to show that if the way to obtain eternal life was easily available at first, from now on it must be sought. The Tree of Life is Jesus because a tree is a symbol of a person (Matt. 3:10; 7:19, 20, and so on). He is the life-giving person. Therefore, the Tree of Life, Jesus, is to be wanted and sought with hard, persistent labor, through the Word, and with the help of God's people.

The Ten Commandments say, "thou shall not kill," and, "thou shall not steal," meaning thou shall not hurt your neighbor. Between the lines, they actually say, "Thou shall love!" When the Lord told Adam not to eat of the forbidden fruit, He actually told him to eat of the other one, the Tree of Life. This they did not understand immediately but only when they realized what they lost.

Jesus said some words that were very disturbing, even among some of His disciples. He invited everybody to eat His flesh and drink His blood (John 6:53–59). Many stumbled at these words, but they meant something else. The word "flesh" is a symbol of His teachings, which are our spiritual food (John 6:45; Matt. 4:4); and His blood is His life, which is our example of living (Lev. 17:11, 14). Do you see how just a quick look at His words could make Jesus seem detestable, but paying close attention to His words gives us a different meaning?

So make sure to pay attention to the words. Your eternal life depends on it.

Elijah the Legacy

A great reformer, greater even than Samuel, was Elijah. From the list of all the prophets, Elijah can be placed next to Moses, not for the same kind of work that Moses did, but for the reform. God set the standard through Moses, but the worship is restored through Elijah. Even though the northern kingdom, namely Israel, chose almost entirely to remain in idolatry, Elijah did everything he could to divert it. His influence penetrated Israel's royal palaces; his messages and rebukes made kings shake like leaves. Many have been encouraged and comforted by his spirit, which moved them to follow him in reforming the people. His spirit influenced even John the Baptist and many others today. Being baptized with water has become a symbol of being baptized with the spirit of Elijah, whereas being baptized with the Holy Spirit means to be baptized with the Spirit of Christ in addition to the spirit of Elijah. His spirit will continue to influence many others till the end, till the second coming of Christ. His faith and trust in God were that of a titan, and his love for the Lord and His cause was untroubled. Even though he built a reputation worthy to be envied and left behind such a legacy, he was not a god as many of his time thought him to be. He was just like you and me—100 percent human.

In this chapter I try my best to show the humanity of Elijah, as I have shown it already in previous chapters, in contrast with God's unchanging love and patience with his elect servants. This will help us better understand His love in His dealings with Elijah. So please give me a chance, and hear me out because what you are about to discover has never been shared before, and it will shake your very foundation of biblical knowledge. I am not trying to scare anyone but to encourage through an introduction to a new revolution in Bible study. Jesus started it with His Sermon on the Mount, as I have shown in previous chapters, and I am only following in His footsteps (Matt. 5:31, 32, 38, 39). He gave us a hint, and I am digging deeper into it, trying to develop every detail possible. So help me God!

There is one major event from the Elijah's life that I want to analyze with you. It is perhaps the most difficult to explain and the most important from his life, and it is found in 1 Kings 18:20–40. It describes Elijah's victory over the prophets of Baal. The reader should inform himself or herself of the passage. There, on Mount Carmel, a debate took place in which Elijah, God's prophet, challenged the prophets of Baal to prove which god was the real God. The challenge was to show which god would answer by sending fire upon their sacrifices (1 Kings 18:23, 24). The prophets of Baal started first with no result after a long day of agonizing rituals calling unto their god, Baal. Elijah followed after them by preparing his sacrifice with a lot of water to make it look more challenging (vs. 33–35). After a short prayer that he addressed to his God, fire came down, consuming the sacrifice, the wood, the stones, the dust, and, "licked up the water that was in the trench" (v. 38). When all the people saw this, "they fell on their faces: and they said, The Lord, he is the God; the Lord, he is the God" (v. 39).

I have listened to sermons describing this event so many times, and I always thought that the preachers had it right; the Lord was the One who answered by fire at Elijah's prayer. It even says so in verse 38. Today, for the first-time ever, I present evidence to show all those who love God's Word that Satan will always be present with God's servants and will always look for opportunities in which he can deceive even the very elect to the point where he is allowed to bring even fire in the name of the Lord. But he will use that to create an emotion far from genuine for the benefit of deceit. I know this is very difficult to grasp. That is why I left the best for last. But please give me a chance to explain.

From the start, the record introduces Elijah as he is going to King Ahab to rebuke him (1 Kings 17:1). He is obviously sent by the Lord, but he is exalting God and himself at the same time, as if he wants to make sure that Ahab knows who Elijah is and that he should not be taken for granted. Elijah is not just anybody but the only one. He is very proud of his mission.

After three years and a half, Elijah is commanded by the Lord to go and show himself to King Ahab so that He can send rain upon the earth. We do not have any proof that the Lord told him to challenge the prophets of Baal on Mount Carmel the way he did in chapter 18. This he must have planned on his own. Through his plan he meant well, but our plans, no matter how good they may seem, are not always in accordance with His will (Isa. 55:8, 9). So as long as we don't have the evidence that the Lord told him so, we cannot assume that. Verse 1 from 1 Kings chapter 18 is all that we have as the commandment of the Lord. If the Lord commanded that challenge of Elijah, then we need the evidence. Besides, why would God have Elijah bring a sacrifice when Elijah was not a priest? We don't have any evidence that he was born from the genealogy of Aaron. God Himself commanded that only the priests should bring the sacrifices and only on the altar before the tabernacle (Lev. 17:3, 4; Deut. 12:4–6, 11, 13, 14; 1 Sam. 13: 9–14). God does not violate His own word, so He could not have commanded Elijah to do something wrong that would inspire others to do so also.

There are, however, two cases in the book of Judges where we have two individuals who were not priests but brought sacrifices on God's commandment. These accounts are found in Judges 6:17–24 and in Judges 13:15–23. They describe how the Lord allowed these men to bring sacrifices. Let the reader not forget that during the time of the judges, "every man did that which was right in his own eyes" (Judges 17:6; 21:25). Moses warned them against it (Deut. 12:

8). Chaos and anarchy were the order in Israel, and because of that, the Lord made some exceptions by His grace. These men did not bring sacrifices publicly but privately. And in both cases, we have the direct word of the Lord as evidence that He allowed them to do that. In Elijah's case, we only have an assumption. In Elijah's time the temple had been built and the priesthood and the Levitical orders were in place and fully functional. There was no excuse.

The only hint we have about a possible command from the Lord is found in Elijah's prayer in 1 Kings 18:36: "Lord God of Abraham, Isaac, and of Israel, let it be known this day that thou art God in Israel, and that I am thy servant, and that I have done all these things at thy word." So Elijah hints toward a possible command that he might have received from the Lord, but it does not stand the biblical test. Just as we have done in every chapter so far, the same we will do here. Maybe somebody did command Elijah to bring the sacrifice, but was it from the Lord? This dilemma needs an answer. We will study Elijah's behavior and actions to see if the Lord, or someone else, was leading him entirely because every servant of God has to walk according, "to the law and to the testimony: if they speak not according to this word, it is because there is no light in them" (Isa. 8:20).

When he meets Elisha for the first time, Elijah behaves arrogantly with him. Elisha asks him if he can go and kiss his parents goodbye, and then he will follow Elijah (1 Kings 19:19, 20). Elijah replies, "Go back again: for what have I done to thee?" What Elijah is saying is, "Don't you know who I am? I am calling you in the name of the Lord. If you don't appreciate it, then go back to your business." What Elijah was saying was correct. Jesus, on one occasion, answered one of His followers in a similar way when He was asked the same question Elisha asked Elijah (Luke 9:61, 62). The difference is that Jesus answered His follower in a humbler and more polite manner than Elijah did. Elijah was being taken by a proud spirit.

When Obadiah, the governor of the house of Ahab, met Elijah, "he fell on his face," meaning he worshipped Elijah (1 Kings 18:7).

Elijah should not have accepted Obadiah's obeisance. When Cornelius saw Peter, he fell down at his feet and worshipped him (Acts 10:25, 26). In response, Peter raised him up and said, "Stand up; I myself also am a man." The apostle John did the same to an angel, and the angel forbade him to do so (Rev. 19:10; 22:8, 9). This made Elijah boastful to a certain degree.

At the time when the prophets of Baal were calling unto their god to answer by fire, Elijah mocked them and their rituals (1 Kings 18:27). Jesus never did anything similar to that. After the fire that came down from heaven had consumed Elijah's sacrifice, he commanded the seizing of Baal's prophets and, "slew them" (1 Kings 18:40). He did not even give them a chance to repent. Maybe some of them would have admitted that they had been wrong and may have repented. But no! To Elijah, they were ripe for destruction.

Right after the killing of Baal's prophets, Elijah went to the top of Mount Carmel to pray for the rain (1 Kings 18:41–45). There he had to pray seven times before the Lord finally answered to his prayer. When Elijah prayed for the fire to come down upon his sacrifice, the fire descended immediately. He received an answer to a plan that we do not have evidence that was devised by the Lord. And here he had to insist seven times on asking the Lord to answer to a plan for which we have evidence that was devised by the Lord. Strange, isn't it? It's as if somebody else answered him with fire. And speaking of answering with fire, we proved in previous chapters that the Lord, at Mount Horeb, taught Elijah that God does not answer with fire, wind, and earthquake (1 Kings 19:11, 12).

Before he decided to go to Mount Horeb, while he was running away from Jezebel, an angel met him and comforted him in the wilderness (1 Kings 19:4–8). As Elijah was sleeping, the angel touched him and told him to rise and eat. He found a "cake" and a "cruse of water." He ate and drank and went back to sleep. The angel came again the second time, "touched him, and said, Arise and eat; because the journey is too great for thee." He got up, ate, and drank, and decided to go to Mount Horeb. When he got there, the Lord asked, "What doest thou here, Elijah?" (1 Kings 19:9). In other words, the Lord asks him, "Who called you here, Elijah? What business do you have here?" Isn't that strange? The angel never told him to go to Mount Horeb; the angel only told him to eat and drink because the journey was too great for him. What journey? The angel was speaking symbolically. His life's journey was too great for him, his work, and his mission. The angel offered him food and water so that Elijah would receive comfort because he said in his prayer that he felt alone and wanted to die (1 Kings 19:4). He repeated that in verse 10 and 14, which means that he was really desperate. God never called him to Mount Horeb, so Elijah misunderstood the words of the angel. The angel was assuring him that, in his mission, he was not alone, even though he felt alone. Either Elijah assumed that the angel was telling him to go to Mount Horeb, or Satan was whispering to him that the Lord was calling him there, to get him far away from his mission. This needed to be cleared once and for all.

When God allowed the fire to pass before Elijah, I believe that He was making a special reference to that event that happened on Mount Carmel, a plan devised by Elijah without asking the Lord. God was telling him, "I was not the One who sent the fire on Mount Carmel." It is possible that somebody did tell him to bring a sacrifice, but it was definitely not the Lord. Satan saw the opportunity and acted promptly. Elijah told the people that he did everything (the sacrifice) according to the Word of the Lord, and the Lord told Elijah that He was not the author of that plan and of that fire.

If Elijah was wrong and made a mistake, then why did the Lord listen to him and give rain? Because the people needed it. It is exactly as when Moses sinned in the wilderness when he spoke rashly and hit the rock twice instead of once. But the Lord still listened to him and gave water to the people because they needed it (Numbers 20:1–13).

People love to see such powerful manifestations of the supernatural, which create false emotions but not true conversions. The Jews were always tempting Jesus to give them a sign by performing a miracle, and in response, they would believe in Him

(Matt. 12:38; 16:1; Mark 8:11; John 6:30). Jesus never fulfilled their lust for false emotions. This is what God was trying to make Elijah understand: "Don't plan such challenges anymore, and if anybody asks for a sign, tell them that God is in a 'still small voice'," meaning words of wisdom, parables, or in other words, His Word, the Holy Scriptures.

Elijah loved God, and God loved Elijah. The Lord loves us in the same manner. The Lord had patience with Elijah because He worked with what He had. Elijah consecrated himself to the Lord for his people, and the Lord used him because he was all He had. Elijah made one great mistake; He trusted the Lord like a titan but neglected His ceremonial law. We do not have any evidence that he visited the temple in Jerusalem. Every male was required to visit the temple at least three times a year. This means that he never brought a sacrifice for his own sins. Yet because of the deep idolatry in Israel, the Lord understood him, forgave him, and took him to heaven. Through this very act, by taking Elijah to heaven, the Lord tells us, "This is what I want and this is what I expect from all of you. As Elijah gave his 100 percent to Me, the same I expect from you." My 100 percent might not be the same as Elijah's 100 percent. Some are capable of more, others of less. But don't worry. Just like Elijah, we will be saved by grace. Grace will supply what we lack because of our mistakes and misunderstandings, but not if we rebel. The spirit of Elijah is a symbol of total trust, pure faith, that leads to salvation by grace. Amen!

Addendum
Revelation 8:1

I came across an interesting discovery in my studies and would like to share it with you. It is found in Revelation 8:1. It's a study that requires your very careful attention. It is a prophecy regarding our spiritual preparation in the near future. This is what the verse says: "And when he had opened the seventh seal, there was silence in heaven about the space of half an hour." We will prove again that the language of this paragraph is not literal but symbolic.

"He" who opens the seal is the Lamb, or Jesus, as He is seen in chapter 5 at the beginning of the seals of the book that He opens. A "seal" of the book is a period of time specified by the book. The seventh seal is the last period of the church. "Silence" is a symbol for death or corruption (Ps. 31:17; 94:17; 115:17, check margin; Isa. 15:1; Jer. 8:14). "Heaven" is a symbol for the kingdom of heaven, the church (Matt. 3:2; 4:17; 10:7; Mark 1:14, 15).

It is impossible to have a period of thirty minutes of total silence in heaven, where everybody keeps his or her mouth shut and makes no noise, to keep silence. It makes no sense. But if we can have a symbolic period of spiritual death or corruption in the church on earth, then we're on to something that makes more sense. So, what is "half an hour," and when is its starting point? "Hour" is a symbol of time (Matt. 9:22; 15:28; 17:18; 24:42; 26:40, 45; Mark 14:35; Luke 10:21; 22:14, 53; John 2:4; 4:21, 23; 5:25, 28; 7: 30; 8:20; 12:23, 27;

13:1; 16:21, 32; 17: 1; 19:27; and so on). A time represents a year. The only reference we have about this is in "Antiquities of the Jews", book 10, where Josephus, a very trusted historian, writes about the "seven times" prophesied by Daniel to Nebuchadnezzar (Daniel 4:25) as being seven literal years. During these years, King Nebuchadnezzar had lost his reason (Daniel 4:16, 23–check margin).

One year was always considered to have 360 days. Therefore, we can consider that "half an hour" is 360/2 = 180 prophetic days. One prophetic day equals one literal year (Num. 14:34; Ezek. 4:6). So there will be 180 years of spiritual death or corruption in the church. If we can find the starting point, then we'll know exactly when they will end.

Daniel 8:14 says, "And he said unto me, Unto two thousand and three hundred days; then shall the sanctuary be cleansed." The reader should know that this verse is also symbolic and should be interpreted accordingly. "The sanctuary" represents the church (2 Thess. 2:4; Hebrews 3:5, 6). A sanctuary is a temple and a house. Using the 1 day = 1 year interpretation, then 2,300 days = 2,300 years. The "cleansing of the sanctuary" means the purification process of God's people, and he does that process with fire, meaning with persecution (2 Tim. 3:12). So translating this verse would sound something like this: Until 2,300 years, and then shall the purifying persecution cease. If we could find the starting point of this prophecy, then we could find the starting point of the one from Revelation 8:1. I will show you how.

In Daniel chapter 9, we have what is called the, "seventy weeks prophecy," in verse 24. "Seventy weeks are determined upon thy people". The word "determined" is *nechtak* in Hebrew and actually means to cut from a portion, and not to determine. Therefore, seventy weeks were cut from a larger portion, larger than seventy weeks or 490 years (70 x 7 = 490, using 1 day = 1 year). From what portion were these 490 years cut? From the 2,300 years.

Acquaint yourself with the book of Daniel because the 2,300-day prophecy is the biggest in that book and also the main one from chapters 8 to 12. Everything in those chapters happens within the 2,300 day/year prophecy. Therefore, the 70 weeks, or 490 years, are the first portion being cut from the 2,300 years, and they were assigned to the Jewish people, the people of Daniel. When did they start? The next verse, verse 25, describes that: "Know therefore and understand, that from the going forth of the commandment to restore and to build Jerusalem unto the Messiah the Prince shall be seven weeks, and threescore and two weeks: the street shall be built again, and the wall, even in troublous times." The commandment in discussion here is found in Ezra 7:1–28. There, King Artaxerxes gives a letter containing a decree, or a "commandment" to establish the state of Israel back to its original position. To "restore Jerusalem" means to restore the capital, therefore restoring the state of Israel. This decree was given in 457 BC, "in the seventh year of Artaxerxes" (v. 8). Artaxerxes the Great, or Longimanus, started to reign in 464 BC (check Ptolemy's *Canon of Kings*). So using 457 BC, his seventh year, as the starting point and adding 2,300 years, we get 1,843 (2,300 – 457 = 1,843). So AD 1843 is when the church worldwide was free from persecution.

There's always and there will always be persecution on a personal level, but it refers to a worldwide persecution, which the church has gone through since 457 BC until the Catholic persecution, which was the longest and the cruelest. If the church was cleansed in AD 1843, then that's when the church felt at ease and entered a period of relaxation and spiritual corruption that is obvious even to the atheistic world. Adding 180 years to it would bring us to year AD 2023. This is the year Revelation 8:1 says spiritual death and corruption will end, meaning that a great awakening will take place.

This is how I think the awakening will take place; by the way, it is only a personal opinion. If there's an awakening, then there's a persecution. If there's a persecution, then we won't have any more rights. If we have no more rights, then the Constitution of the United States will be abolished. If the constitution is abolished, then there's no more United States of America. If there's no more

United States, then no other country or institution will be able to protect human rights worldwide. Then a worldwide persecution might start, leading to anarchy and barbarianism. But don't worry. Jesus Christ will return to put an end to that persecution from which none escape.

I'm not trying to predict the second coming of Christ; that cannot be predicted (Mark 13:32). I only discovered a great awakening predicted in the Bible, and I wanted to share it with you. If I'm wrong in my interpretation, then may the Lord forgive me in His great mercy. But what if I'm right?

Printed in the United States
By Bookmasters